Praise for *Intentions at Work*

"Spirituality is about simplicity and this little book is full of simple, practical and spiritual wisdom that has the power to transform your work and your workplace."

Judi Neal, PhD, President & CEO
International Center for Spirit at Work

"Ann Ranson has given simple, yet insightful ways to bring this essential topic into corporate America."

Patricia Aburdene
Author of "Megatrends 2010, The Rise of Conscious Capitalism"
Champion of Corporate Transformation

"Understanding and implementing the ideas, strategies and tools in Ann Ranson's Intentions at Work *is the surest way to create an unfair advantage. Certainly a 'must-read' for anyone involved in today's competitive business environment."*

Martin Howey, CEO
TopLine Business Solutions

"Read this book and take it to heart if you want to be truly happy at work. The tools are simple, yet powerful when used to bring meaning and values to the office. Based on the case studies we're seeing, Ann Ranson has hit the nail on the head with Intentions at Work. *Even corporate leaders are finding that employees are more creative and productive when their spiritual principles are supported and empowered."*

Rebecca Maddox, CEO
Maddox Smye LLC

"Intentions at Work is a potent guidebook that every company needs for those days when stress is high and deadlines are looming."

Richard Feller,
President and CEO
Lynchval Systems Worldwide, Inc.

INTENTIONS
AT
WORK

~

83 Spiritual Tools
To Succeed In
Business

ANN RANSON

Intentions at Work

83 Spiritual Tools to Succeed in Business

Ann Ranson

Published by:
Intentions Work
www.intentionswork.com

Printed in the United States of America

Cover design: Michael Blank, The D Group, Dallas, TX
www.thedgroup.com

ISBN: 978-0-9798188-0-6

To
CARLA AND MARY

Acknowledgements

Prior to launching Intentions Work in 2005,
I worked in the corporate world for over 25
years as a sales and marketing professional.
During these years I learned from the people
that I worked with – sometimes I learned
what to do and sometimes what not to do –
both being equally valuable! I won't list names,
because the list would be exhaustive!
Suffice it to say, I've been blessed to attract
smart, creative, compassionate, innovative,
and interesting people – men, women, younger,
older – with all kinds of titles, whether receptionist,
assistant or CEO – I have learned from them all.

Everything you read here is the integration of
a lifetime of learning. I want to thank all of my
business colleagues, my family and my friends
who have touched my life in some way. I truly
appreciate all of it.

A special thanks to Michael Blank, my graphic
designer - The D Group - for his generous and
continual help. I couldn't have done it without you.

And to my son Taylor, an extra special thanks for
his treasured support and belief in me.
What an inspiration he is!

Introduction

Maybe you've felt a desire to bring more of your authentic, spiritual self into your business, but weren't sure where to begin. You may also have been concerned about how to address issues about separation of work and spirituality. Let me first assure you that bringing spirituality into the workplace is easier than you may think, because it is NOT about religion, dogma or walking a certain path. It IS about human kindness, trust and values. As many Americans spend increasingly more time at work, maybe it's natural to want more spiritual support at work. Possibly the increased stress in your daily work life creates the need and desire for a more acknowledged connection to your Higher Power.

Whatever it is that calls you to more fully express your values and live them wherever you are, _Intentions at Work_ is designed to give you simple tools that you can begin using today. They give you an instant point of focus, centered in the belief that there is a Higher Power present in every part of the universe, including work. Many of the tools are accompanied by an inspiring quote to help you go deeper into the spiritual tool to find your own meaning and direction. Others offer suggestions, resources or research to give you a greater understanding of the principle.

There are many ways to get the benefit from this powerful resource. You may:

• Use this book each morning as you arrive at work to set a positive and spiritual tone for the day.
• Start at #1 and read one each day in sequential order.
• Randomly open the book each day to discover which message jumps out to greet you.
• Keep it on your desk for a quick "pick me up" or for others to scan while waiting in your office.
• Use it as a workbook by
- Writing in your journal to reflect on the meaning you derive from each tool.
- Making notes on each page with action steps you can take to incorporate the tool.
• Take one tool at a time, working to master it before moving on to the next.

Any way you decide to use _Intentions at Work_ will be the perfect way for you to connect to your true spiritual nature. Enhance your workplace to create an environment rich with spiritual principles by sharing these tools with your colleagues, your supervisors and your employees. Make the ideas contagious and see what can happen!

Please write to me at 83Tools@intentionswork.com to share your favorite ways to use _Intentions at Work_. They may be featured in future editions of _Intentions at Work_.

*D*oing your best work
feeds your soul
and
your wallet.

~

"The dictionary is the only place where success comes before work."

Vince Lombardi

Don't proselytize.

~

"Spirituality in business is not about religion or dogma,
it's about integrity, trust and values."

Ann Ranson

_S_tate a positive intention at the beginning of each day or week.

For example:
"Today I solve problems with grace and ease."

---

*U*nderstand the motives for the words you speak and the actions that you take. Your motives will reveal the truth.

~)

"Don't let your ego get too close to your position, so that if your position gets shot down, your ego doesn't go with it."

Colin Powell

Assess and acknowledge your strengths so that you can expand them.

~

"To spur high-margin growth and thereby increase their value, great organizations need only focus inward to find the wealth of unrealized capacity that resides in every single employee."

Marcus Buckingham

*K*now what you stand for so that you know which choices to make.

~

"Let the world know you as you are, not as you think you should be, because sooner or later, if you are posing, you will forget the pose, and then where are you?"

Fanny Brice

*F*ind ways to connect to
the world and the colleagues
around you.
Know that you are a part
of a bigger vision.

~

"We cannot live only for ourselves.
A thousand fibers connect us with our fellow men."

Herman Melville

*B*reathe deeply to release stress and to connect to your heart.

~

"Breathe. Let go. And remind yourself that
this very moment is the only one
you know you have for sure."

Oprah Winfrey

*L*ook for opportunities
to be of service and know
that the more you give
the more you receive.

~

"Teach this triple truth to all:
A generous heart, kind speech, and a life of service
and compassion are the things which renew humanity."

Buddha

Use the golden rule.

~

"The golden rule for every business man is this:
'Put yourself in your customer's place.'"

Dr. Orison Sweet Marden

*R*emember there is a
Higher Power at work in every
situation, no matter how
it looks at the moment.

⁓

"Everything exists for some reason as part of
the perfect intelligence that is the universe."

Dr. Wayne Dyer

*S*tay focused on what's
really important.
Release the petty stuff.
Ask yourself, "is this
really important"?

"You have to trust your inner knowing.
If you have a clear mind...you won't have
to search for direction. Direction will come to you."

Phil Jackson

Have a plan for what you want to accomplish, then act with confidence.

~

"If your actions inspire others to dream more, earn more, do more and become more, you are a leader."

John Quincy Adams

*L*ook for opportunities
to show compassion.
It is the greatest gift of all.

~

"Our task must be to free ourselves by widening
our circle of compassion to embrace all living
creatures and the whole of nature and its beauty."

Albert Einstein

---

*S*tart each work day
with a moment of
silence.

~

"Silence is the mother of truth."

Benjamin Disraeli

*A*ffiliate with positive,
caring colleagues:
the energy you create
together will heal many
situations.

~

"I'm not the smartest fellow in the world,
but I can sure pick smart colleagues."

Franklin D. Roosevelt

To live in balance,
concentrate on work at work;
play and rest at home.

"The best and safest thing is to keep a balance in
your life, acknowledge the great powers around us
and in us. If you can do that, and live that way,
you are really a wise man."

Euripides

*S*upport negative people
from a distance so
you don't get caught
in their energy.

~

"Be careful the environment you choose for it will
shape you; be careful the friends you choose
for you will become like them."

W. Clement Stone

---

*E*ncourage creativity
and allow ones the
freedom to fail.

~

"Creativity is piercing the mundane to find the marvelous."

Bill Moyers

*D*on't gossip;
use mothers rule:
If you can't say something nice,
don't say anything at all!

~

"Wise men speak because they have something to say;
fools, because they have to say something."

Plato

*O*ffering praise sincerely and frequently helps everyone succeed.

~

"Most of us, swimming against the tides of trouble the world knows nothing about, need only a bit of praise or encouragement - and we will make the goal."

Robert Collier

*B*e holistic in your approach
to business and know
you can integrate spirituality
and business.

~

"Magic happens at the intersection of profits and people,
head and heart and intellect and intuition."

Ann Ranson

When problems arise,
take a moment alone
to get still, ask for clarity,
then listen for guidance.

"Listen to those inner signals that help you make the right choices – no matter what anyone else thinks."

Dr. Wayne Dyer

$\mathcal{F}$ind ways to innovate:
the creativity that erupts
will exhilarate you.

∽

"Just because something doesn't do what you
planned it to do doesn't mean it's useless."

Thomas A. Edison

*L*ook for the lesson –
then learn it!
PS:
There's always
a lesson.

"The only things worth learning are the things
you learn after you know it all."

Harry S. Truman

*L*aunch a book club
featuring positive, empowering
and thought-provoking books.

See the resource section at the back of this book
for a list to get you started.

_Q_uit whining
and everyone will
thank you.

~

"If you listen to your fears, you will die never knowing
what a great person you might have been."

Robert H. Schuller

*O*ffer or organize enrichment programs that support and expand your teams.

How about yoga, meditation, dance, exercise, nutrition or personal development courses?

When you let go
of resistance, the power
of ease moves in to
take its' place.

⌣

"Through the years of experience I have found that
air offers less resistance than dirt."

Jack Nicklaus

*I*f you can't love your job, know there is a perfect place for you somewhere else.

"If you cannot work with love but only with distaste, it is better that you should leave your work."

Kahlil Gibran

*R*emember…
all people are equal,
no matter what title they
hold (at the moment).

~

"I believe that every person is born with talent."

Maya Angelou

*O*ffer advice sparingly.

~

"Wise men don't need advice. Fools won't take it."

Benjamin Franklin

_E_veryday, find something to
be grateful for – as you look,
you'll find more to
be grateful for.

~

"Develop an attitude of gratitude, and give thanks
for everything that happens to you, knowing that
every step forward is a step toward achieving something
bigger and better than your current situation."

Brian Tracy

*B*e humble,
which means to
be teachable.

~

"The humble improve"

Wynton Marsalis

_T_ake total responsibility
for your work and
your attitude.

~

"Too many leaders act as if the sheep...
their people... are there for the benefit of the shepherd,
not that the shepherd has responsibility for the sheep."

Ken Blanchard

Start a "Chicken Soup for the Soul at Work" group.

~

"We are working souls - loving, growing, always evolving - 'doing the best we can'".

from Introduction to "Chicken Soup for the Soul at Work"

Create a sacred or quiet space in your office.

~

"Learn to be quiet enough to hear the genuine within yourself so that you can hear it in others."

Marian Wright Edelman

Be ethical.

~

"Integrity is the essence of everything successful."

Buckminster Fuller

*P*rofits grow when you see
vendors and customers
as allies instead
of adversaries.

~

"Unity is strength... when there is teamwork and
collaboration, wonderful things can be achieved."

Mattie Stepanek

*T*rue power gives
freedom to all, so think
how you can empower
those around you.

~

"I hope our wisdom will grow with our power,
and teach us, that the less we use our power
the greater it will be."

Thomas Jefferson

*S*et a tone of integrity
and watch others
rise to your level.

~

"Have the courage to say no. Have the courage to
face the truth. Do the right thing because it is right.
These are the magic keys to living your life with integrity."

W. Clement Stone

Knowledge comes
from all senses –
stay open and do not
limit yourself.

~

"Knowledge comes, but wisdom lingers."

Alfred Lord Tennyson

*W*hen you walk
your talk,
people will
naturally follow.

~

"Conscience is the authentic voice of God to you."

Rutherford B. Hayes

*B*uild a team to
harness the creativity
and wisdom of all.

⌣

"Teamwork is so important that it is virtually impossible
for you to reach the heights of your capabilities or
make the money that you want without becoming
very good at it."

Brian Tracy

*O*ffer paid days off from work for community service plus days off for mental health.

"For it is in giving that we receive."

St. Francis of Assisi

*H*ave a positive
and personal vision
for your work.

~

"Your vision will become clear only when you can
look into your own heart. Who looks outside, dreams;
who looks inside, awakes."

Carl Jung

Act on what you
believe is right or
where your passion
leads you.

~

"Most of the important things in the world have been
accomplished by people who have kept on trying when
there seemed to be no hope at all."

Dale Carnegie

Acknowledge accomplishments, big and small, yours and others.

~

"The best and safest thing is to keep a balance in your life, acknowledge the great powers around us and in us. If you can do that, and live that way, you are really a wise man."

Euripides

*A*void energy and time leaks to maintain your focus and passion.

~

"When mental energy is allowed to follow the line of least resistance and to fall into easy channels, it is called weakness."

James Allen

*B*e willing to
stand alone for what
you believe is important.

~

"Be who you are and say what you feel because
those who mind don't matter and those
who matter don't mind."

Dr Seuss

What you can conceive, you can achieve. Believe it!

~

"Think of yourself as on the threshold of unparalleled success. A whole, clear, glorious life lies before you. Achieve! Achieve!"

Andrew Carnegie

To live the life
you want, be intentional
in everything you do and say.

"Intention mindfully; you must be able to detach
from the outcome, and let the universe handle the
details of fulfillment."

Deepak Chopra

Fifty-three

*L*ighten up and
don't take yourself
or others too seriously.

⌣

"Your attitude is like a box of crayons that color
your world. Constantly color your picture gray, and
your picture will always be bleak. Try adding some
bright colors to the picture by including humor,
and your picture begins to lighten up."

Allen Kloin

*O*wn your opinions,
then voice your opinions
in a considerate and
positive way.

~

"One of the greatest feelings in life is the conviction that
you have lived the life you wanted to life – with the rough
and the smooth, the good and the bad – but yours,
shaped by your own choices, and not someone else's."

Michael Ignatieff

Commit to a cause that feeds your soul.

~

"One of the best kept secrets in America is that people are aching to make a commitment, if they only had the freedom and environment in which to do so."

John Naisbitt

*I*f you feel afraid,
remember fear is
only **F**alse **E**vidence
Appearing **R**eal.

"We gain strength, and courage, and confidence by
each experience in which we really stop to look
fear in the face... we must do that which we think
we cannot."

Eleanor Roosevelt

Believe that you
can make a difference;
in fact you already do.

⁓

"Be the change you wish to see in the world."

Mahatma Gandhi

Let go of prejudices.

~

"Prejudice is a burden that confuses the past, threatens the future and renders the present inaccessible."

Maya Angelou

---

*O*rganize a think tank
that meets regularly to
consider the possibilities.

~

"To achieve, you need thought. You have to know
what you are doing and that's real power."

Ayn Rand

Make socially responsible purchasing decisions at work.

~

Over 50% of the adult population report that their values influence some or most of their purchasing decisions.

*S*how respect
and tolerance
to everyone.

~

"To be one, to be united is a great thing. But to respect
the right to be different is maybe even greater."

Bono

*F*requently and consistently share the company vision, then engage the team to bring it to life.

~

"A man who has a vision is not able to use the power of it until after he has performed the vision on earth for the people to see."

Black Elk

Look for real solutions for every problem you see.

"Courage means to keep working a relationship, to continue seeking solutions to difficult problems, and to stay focused during stressful periods."

Denis Waitley

*T*hink positive
to have positive results.

⌒

"Shoot for the moon. Even if you miss, you'll land
among the stars."

Les Brown

*D*eliver on your promises. Better yet, OVER deliver on your promises!

"Promises are like crying babies in a theater, they should be carried out at once."

· Norman Vincent Peale

*T*hink of big ideas
your business can use
to make a difference with
customers, employees
& the world.

~

"What's possible exceeds what's impossible"

Mark Victor Hansen

---

*L*ook within to
find your truth.

~

"A man travels the world over in search of what
he needs and returns home to find it."

George Moore

$\mathcal{L}$ook for the good in
everyone and in
every situation -
it is there.

~

"Perpetual optimism is a force multiplier."

Colin Powell

Believe in the mission.

~

"The thing always happens that you really believe in;
and the belief in a thing makes it happen."

Frank Lloyd Wright

Remember your dreams and have a plan to achieve them.

～

"Cherish your visions and your dreams as they are the children of your soul, the blueprints of your ultimate achievements."

Napoleon Hil

*T*ake time every day
to think: open to inspiration
and allow your creativity
to blossom.

"In the rush and noise of life, as you have intervals,
step within yourselves and be still. Wait upon God and
feel His good presence; this will carry you through
your day's business."

William Penn

*T*hink short term
and long term to avoid
surprising changes in
the market.

~

"The fellow that can only see a week ahead is
always a popular fellow, for he is looking with
the crowd. But the one that can see years ahead,
he has a telescope but he can't make anybody
believe that he has it."

Will Rogers

Reward shareholders, employees and customers with corporate philanthropy.

~

"I don't know what your destiny will be, but one thing
I do know: the only ones among you who will be really
happy are those who have sought and found
how to serve."

Albert Schweitzer

Seventy-four

---

*H*onor your
values to build
self-respect.

~

"When your values are clear to you, making
decisions becomes easier."

Roy Disney

*L*ook for work
that feeds your soul.

~

"I think the person who takes a job in order to live -
that is to say, for the money - has turned himself
into a slave."

Joseph Campbell

Remember your Source.

⌣

"The same source that gave you the idea will give you the means to see it through."

Alan Cohen

Embrace growth and change.

~

"Winners must learn to relish change with the same enthusiasm and energy that we have resisted it in the past."

Tom Peters

*B*uild a superior culture by anticipating customer and employee needs.

~

"You have to work at creating your own culture"

Mitch Albom

*F*ollow your gut –
trust it to lead you true.

~

"Nothing can bring you peace but yourself"

Ralph Waldo Emerson

*L*augh at every possible opportunity.

~

"If you can't laugh at yourself,
then who can you laugh at?"

Tiger Woods

*U*nderstand the
energy of money:
it only has the power
that you give it.

~

"There is nothing wrong with men possessing riches.
The wrong comes when riches possess men."

Billy Graham

*Y*ou succeed and have fun when you think outside the box – WAY outside the box!

~

"Birds make great sky-circles of their freedom. How do they learn it? They fall, and falling, they're given wings"

Rumi

*F*orgive everyone,
including yourself.

~

"Forgiveness is a virtue of the brave"

Indira Gandhi

Suggested Reading List:
_____

Megatrends 2010: The Rise of Conscious Capitalism
Patricia Aburdene

Chicken Soup for the Soul at Work
Jack Canfield, Mark Victor Hansen, Martin Rutte

The Heart Aroused
David Whyte

Jesus CEO
Laura Beth Jones

The Diamond Cutter
Geshe Michael Roach

The Tao at Work – On Leading and Following
Stanley M. Herman

ONE: The Art and Practice of Conscious Leadership
Lance Secretan

Awaken Your Heart at Work
Jack Canfield

*Edgewalkers: People & Organizations that Take Risks,
Build Bridges and Break New Ground*
Judi Neal

⁓

Visit **www.intentionswork.com** for updated resources
about spirituality in business.

About Ann Ranson

Ann Ranson believes we need help to stay focused on the truth of who we are and that we are part of a spiritual family. Through her speaking, coaching and writing, she provides important reminders of our divinity.

With purpose and intention, Ann left a very successful sales & marketing career in corporate America in 2005 to start Intentions Work, and began living the life she wanted. Now she uses the Intentions at Work tools every day to maintain the kind of mental, emotional, intellectual and spiritual balance that she seeks.

Over the past 30 years, Ann has worked with hundreds of companies, large and small, in developing processes and strategies that support profits and growth. By helping build successful strategies for her clients, Ann consistently achieved or exceeded goals, leading to greater responsibilities and promotions. Her client list includes such familiar names as

Farmers Insurance	The Hartford	7-11
National City Bank	General Motors	Chevron
State Farm Insurance	DHL	Budweiser

As a respected leader in her field, Ann received recognition and awards including a nomination for an Award of Excellence from American Women in Radio and Television. In 2006, Ann was a featured guest on Embracing the Journey, a noted online radio talk show, and she appeared in Science of Mind Magazine.

According to Ann, "Magic happens at the intersection of profits and people, head and heart and intellect and intuition."

Ann is active in various civic, church and service organizations within her community, and in her spare time, she loves to dance and spend time with her son and dog Sparky.

For more information about Ann and Intentions Work, please visit **www.intentionswork.com**

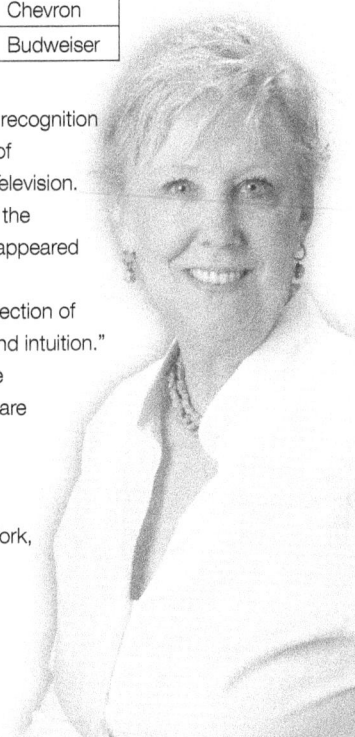

Please Share

INTENTIONS AT WORK
83 Spiritual Tools To Succeed In Business

Intentions at Work: 83 Spiritual Tools to Succeed in Business
is a trademark of Intentions Work and Ann Ranson.

Published by: Intentions Work

Order Information:
Quantity discounts are offered.
Please email *annranson@intentionswork.com*
for pricing information.

To place an order, visit
www.intentionswork.com or **call 972.964.5495**

Notes

Notes

Notes